I LIVE WITH CANCER

WRITTEN BY CHRISTINA EARLEY

ILLUSTRATED BY
AMANDA HUDSON

A Starfish Book

SEAHORSE
PUBLISHING

Teaching Tips for Caregivers:

As a caregiver, you can help your child succeed in school by giving them a strong foundation in language and literacy skills and a desire to learn to read.

This book helps children grow by letting them practice reading skills.

Reading for pleasure and interest will help your child to develop reading skills and will give your child the opportunity to practice these skills in meaningful ways.

- Encourage your child to read on her own at home
- Encourage your child to practice reading aloud
- Encourage activities that require reading
- Establish a reading time
- Talk with your child
- Give your child writing materials

Teaching Tips for Teachers:

Research shows that one of the best ways for students to learn a new topic is to read about it.

Before Reading

- Read the "Words to Know" and discuss the meaning of each word.
- Read the back cover to see what the book is about.

During Reading

- When a student gets to a word that is unknown, ask them to look at the rest of the sentence to find clues to help with the meaning of the unknown word.
- Ask the student to write down any pages of the book that were confusing to them.

After Reading

- Discuss the main idea of the book.
- Ask students to give one detail that they learned in the book by showing a text dependent answer from the book.

TABLE OF CONTENTS

I Live with Cancer

Hi! My name is Luna.

I am seven years old.

I live with my mom, dad, and baby brother
Nick. Nana and Pop Pop live upstairs.

I have **leukemia**. It is a kind of cancer.

6

It makes me **weak** and very tired.
Sometimes, I don't want to eat.

Leukemia is a cancer of the blood.

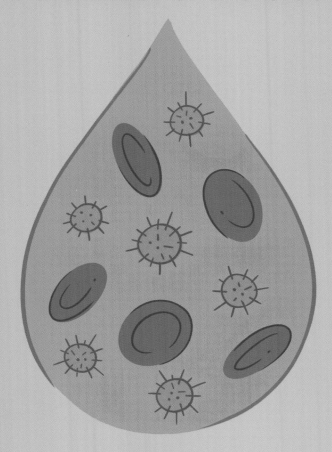

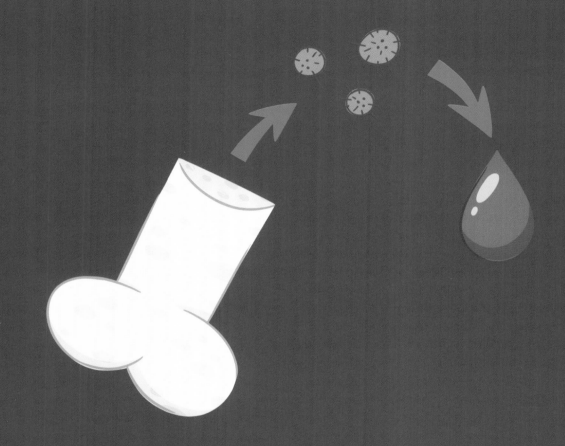

Cancer **cells** get made in **bone marrow**.
Then, they go into the blood.

I go to the hospital for **chemotherapy**.

Rosie makes me feel better.

The treatment makes me lose my hair.

I make sure to use sunscreen when I go outside.

On some days, I can go to school.

My friends there shaved their heads, too!

My favorite subject is science. I like to learn about animals and their habitats.

Mrs. Hobbs teaches us how to make art just like famous artists.

It is fun to make up hula-hoop
games at recess.

My family and I visit the nature center.
Sometimes, I get to feed the raccoons.

When I grow up, I want to be a wildlife doctor.

What do you want to do when you grow up?

LEARN ABOUT CANCER
What Is Cancer?

Cancer is a group of diseases that have to do with cells. Cells are very tiny structures that make up all living things. Each person has billions of cells. When cells that are not normal grow and spread very fast, that is cancer.

Normal cells know when to stop growing. They also die as time passes. But cancer cells keep growing and dividing. They don't die when they are supposed to. Cancer cells make tumors as they grow together in clumps. Tumors destroy healthy cells and can make a person very sick.

Cancer is treated with surgery, chemotherapy, and

radiation. These treatments try to destroy cancer cells. They can cause side effects since healthy cells are also destroyed. Some people experience tiredness and lose their hair. After treatment is over, their energy returns, and their hair grows back. When all signs of cancer are gone from the body, the person is in remission.

Cancer is not contagious. It isn't caused by germs. Doctors aren't sure why some children get cancer and others don't. You can safely talk to, play with, and hug a person with cancer.

Websites to Visit

Alex's Lemonade Stand Foundation: alexslemonade.org
American Childhood Cancer Organization: acco.org
Children's Cancer Network: childrenscancernetwork.org
Sunshine Kids: sunshinekids.org
The National Children's Cancer Society: thenccs.org

Take the Pledge for Inclusion

☑   I accept people of all abilities.

☑   I respect others and act with kindness and compassion.

☑   I include people with special needs and disabilities in my school and in my community.

Get your parent's permission to sign the online pledge at PledgeforInclusion.org.

Famous People Affected by Cancer

Vanessa Bayer: Actor

Sheryl Crow: Musician

Hugh Jackman: Actor

Mario Lemieux: NHL player

Anthony Rizzo: MLB player

Robin Roberts: TV broadcaster

Anthony Rizzo

Robin Roberts

Celebrate and Educate

International Childhood Cancer Day is February 15th.

Childhood Cancer Awareness Month happens in September.

Inclusive Schools Week is the first full week in December.

WORDS TO KNOW

bone marrow (bohn MAR-oh): spongy tissue inside bones

cells (selz): the smallest structures that make up a living thing

chemotherapy (kee-moh-THER-uh-pee): a cancer treatment; using chemicals to destroy cancer cells

leukemia (loo-KEE-mee-uh): cancer of the blood

weak (week): not having enough energy or strength to do things

INDEX

COMPREHENSION QUESTIONS

1. Who lives upstairs in Luna's house?

    a. Rosie

    b. Nana and Pop Pop

    c. Mrs. Hobbs

2. Leukemia is cancer of the _____.

    a. bones

    b. heart

    c. blood

3. What would Luna like to be when she grows up?

    a. a wildlife doctor

    b. a teacher

    c. a baker

4. True or False: Luna can't go to school.

5. True or False: Luna's favorite subject is science.

Answers: 1. b, 2. c, 3. a, 4. False, 5. True

ABOUT THE AUTHOR

Christina Earley lives in sunny south Florida with her son, husband, and rescue dog. She has been teaching children with special needs for over 25 years. She loves to bake cookies, read books about animals, and ride roller coasters.

Written by: Christina Earley
Illustrated by: Amanda Hudson
Design by: Under the Oaks Media
Editor: Kim Thompson

Photos: Conor P. Fitzgerald/Shutterstock: p. 21 (Anthony Rizzo); Leonard Zhukovsky/Shutterstock: p. 21 (Robin Roberts)

Library of Congress PCN Data
I Live with Cancer /Christina Earley
I Live With
ISBN 979-8-8873-5348-7(hard cover)
ISBN 979-8-8873-5433-0(paperback)
ISBN 979-8-8873-5518-4(EPUB)
ISBN 979-8-8873-5603-7(eBook)
Library of Congress Control Number: 2022948887

Printed in the United States of America.

Seahorse Publishing Company

www.seahorsepub.com

Published in the United States
Seahorse Publishing
PO Box 771325
Coral Springs, FL 33077